# Show Me Your Story

## How to Tell Your Life Story with Photos

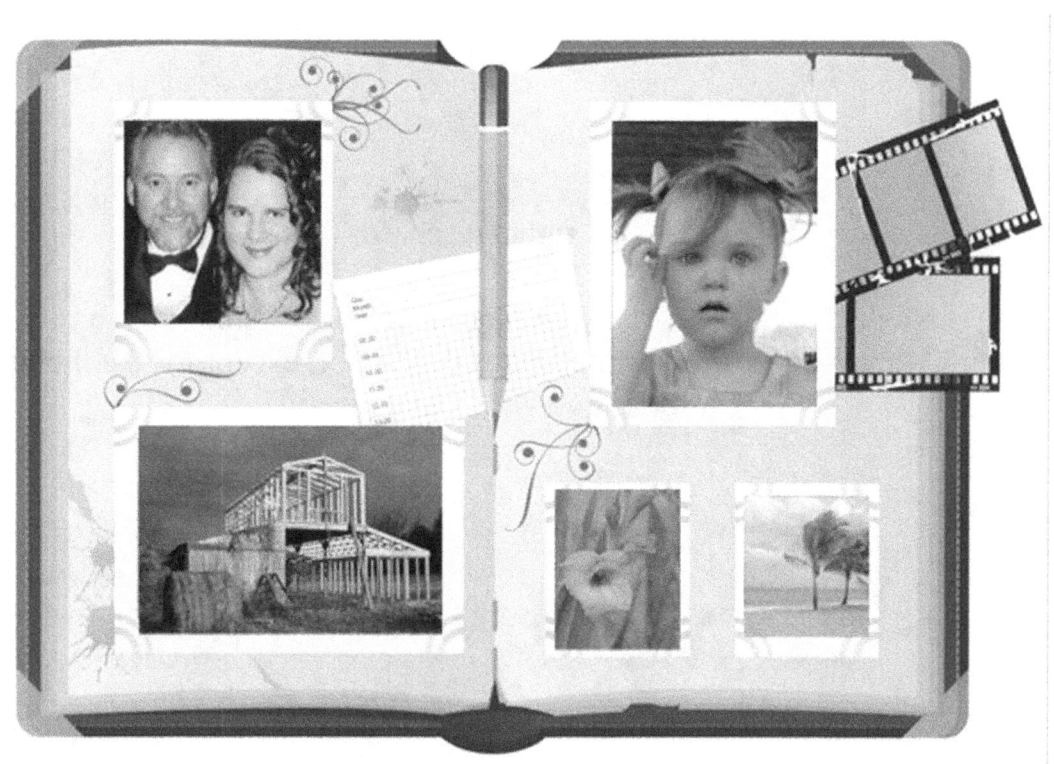

Published by: Photos by Bridget
http://photosbybridget.net
Copyright © 2012 – Bridget Greenwood

Hi my name is Bridget,I am a wife and the mother of 4 children and grandmother of 6 (and counting). I am a hobby photographer and I blog about telling your story with images at http://photosbybridget.net

Like most moms I wanted to capture every little milestone and cute thing that my children did. I come from a family of writers. I don't share their writing talent. With photography I can keep a visual story of my life.

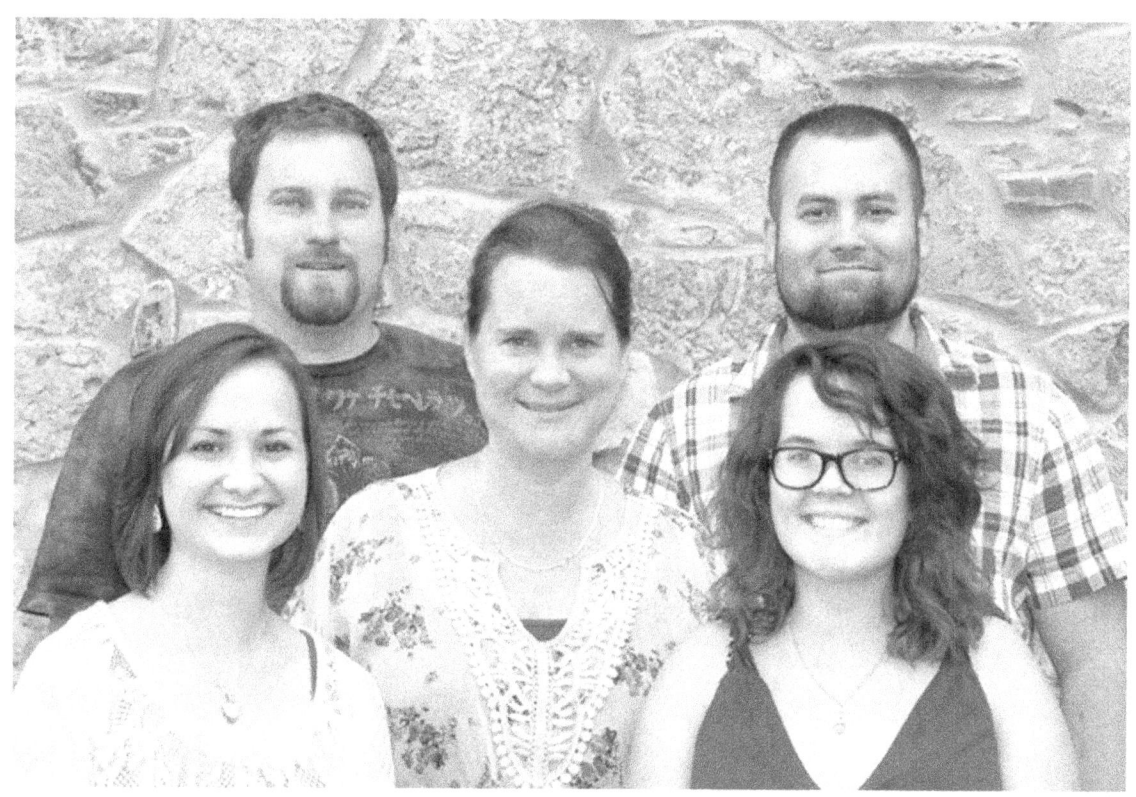

My Kids and I

# Table of Contents

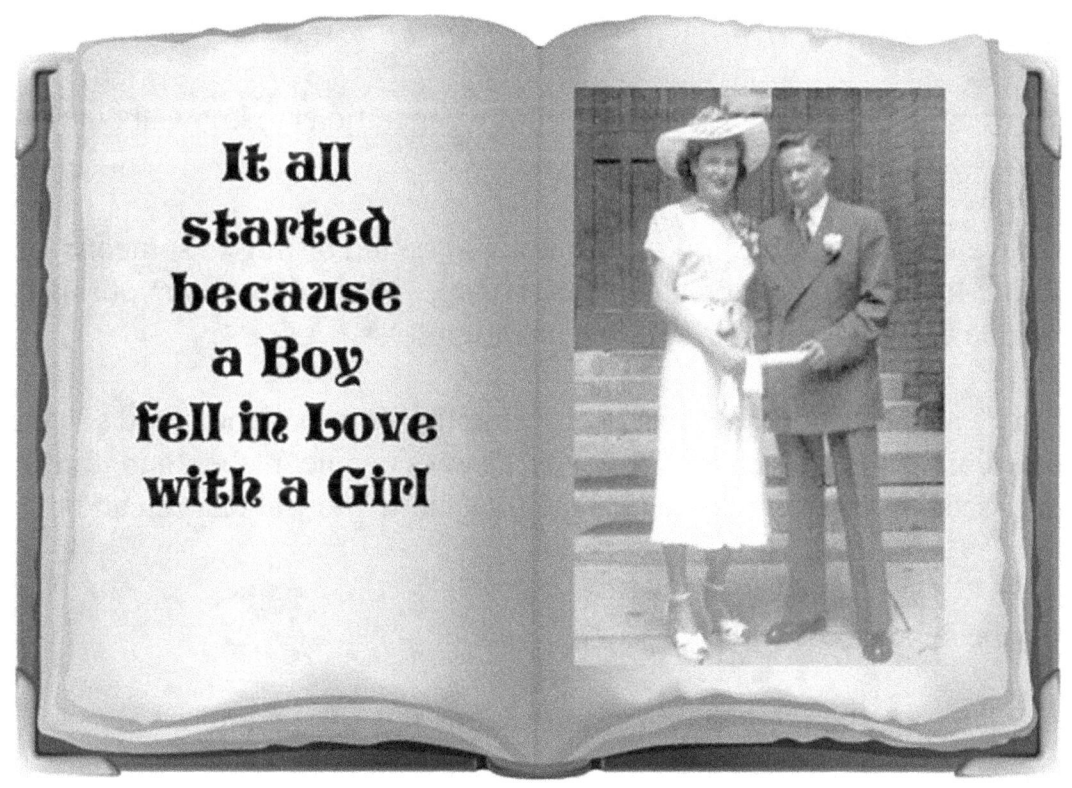

It all
started
because
a Boy
fell in Love
with a Girl

Do You Know Your Grandparents Story?

Will Your Grandchildren Know Yours?

# Why should you tell your story?

*"To be a person is to have a story to tell"* —Isak Dinesen

Writing your own story will make it easier for future generations to know about their great-great grandparents.

You may not have the most interesting story but it will be interesting to someone, especially your family. Your life experiences created who you are, you need to share your life. A life unrecorded can be easily forgotten in future generations.

Telling your story also helps bridge generations, sharing life experiences and showing the differences and similarities in each era. Your story shows people, places, and things someone may have never seen. Your future descendants will want to know about you and the way you lived.

Will your story become a best seller?

Probably not, but to your family and future generations it is something of value.

*"If you don't recount your family history, it will be lost. Honor your own stories and tell them too. The tales may not seem very important, but they are what binds families and makes each of us who we are. "* -Madeleine Engle

# *How Should You Tell* Your Story?

*"When words become unclear, I shall focus with photographs."* *Ansel Adams*

There are many ways to preserve the past for future generations. For me and my family it will be mostly a story told through photos. My grandchildren will be able to look thru our albums and see where we lived, where we vacationed, things we did.

As the old saying goes "a picture is worth a thousand words" Photos help you remember more details when you are trying to write a family history and add more interest.

The more photos you have the less you have to write. Memories fade and it is important to save them, photos keep these memories alive and help you remember.

Tip: Look at your photos closely and get lost in the memory and it will help you write anything the photo is lacking, you can write as much or as little as you think the photo needs to finish telling the story. Photos have the ability to share a feeling and more details than you may be able to describe.

Try to remember the story behind the photos. I use my photos to make simple scrapbooks that tell our family's story. This is not a book about scrapbooking, it is about telling your story using images.

# Moments of Life

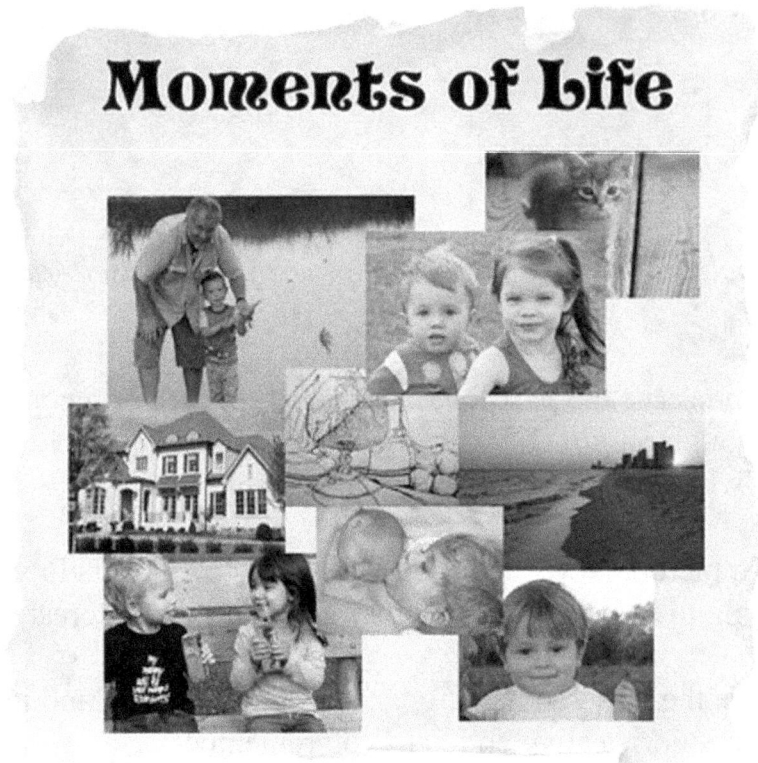

## What Should You Tell In Your Story?

*"Life itself is the most wonderful fairytale of all". —Hans Christian Andersen*

Who you are is affected by where you came from and who your family is so it is important to add a little bit of them to your story. In telling your story you also honor and preserve the stories of your loved ones.

Your story should include your ancestry, your childhood, youth and college. Your mate, children, friends, teams, work, dreams, vacations etc.

You won't be including every little detail of your life, for example don't include every vacation you went on (that is for your photo albums) but you can talk about your favorite vacation spot or if you went to the same place for vacation every year.
Your story is an overall picture of your life, highlighting the milestones and the bigger things, it is not a journal or about the daily little moments of life.

If you have a ton of photo albums like I do you might wonder why you need to create another album. Usually most people will not take the time to sit down and go thru all of your albums, but if you have a story of your life in one album it is much easier to share with others.

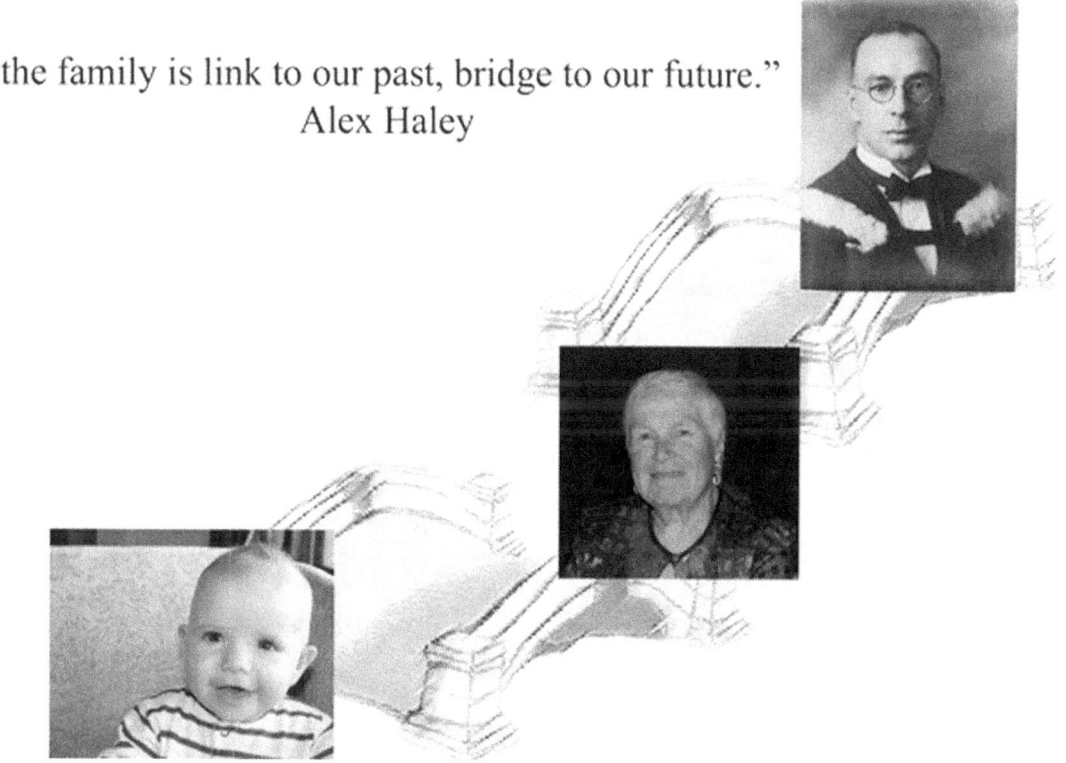

"the family is link to our past, bridge to our future."
Alex Haley

## Ancestry

Even if you never knew them, your ancestors are an important part of your story. Doing a complete in depth ancestry search can be very time consuming and too involved for this project, you will probably just want to add photos or information about your grandparents and great grandparents.

Tip: Add some information, history or photos from the country your ancestors came from.

If you are fortunate enough to know your grandparents ask them about their childhood. Most people love to tell stories of when they were young.
Ask them if they have any photos you can have copied for your story.

Tip: You can create one page and include both sides of the family when creating a page for your grandparents and great grandparents.

Be sure to include any physical traits or things that you have in common, for example my grandmother, mother, me and my children are all computer users. (Someday this will be very common, but in 2012 a lot of older people still don't know how to use a computer.)

Tip: Include the name of your grandparent's children (your aunts and uncles) on their page.

*"Generations pass, like leaves fall from our family tree. Each season new life blossoms and grows, benefiting from the strength and experience of those who went before." -Heidi Swapp*

## Questions:

Do you know what country your ancestors are from?

Where did your grandparents grow up? In the city or the country?

Did Your grandmother work outside the home?

What did your grandfather do?

Did they go to school in a 1 room school house or a large school?

How far did they go in school?

Did they live thru any life changing world events or inventions?

Were they in the military?

Does your family have stories or recipes that have been passed down from generation to generation?

Tip: If you don't have any photos, cook the family recipe and include the photos with the recipe and story on a page.

Were you close to your grandparents?

*If you are interested in learning more about doing your own genealogy research, my grandmother has written a beginner's guide available for sale on Amazon as either an ebook or a physical copy. Beginner's Guide to Genealogy Research by Eleanor McCallum*

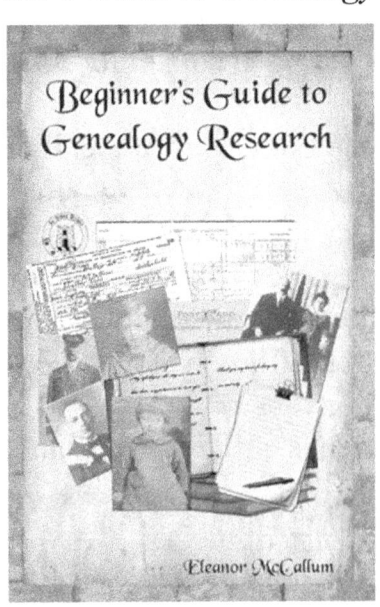

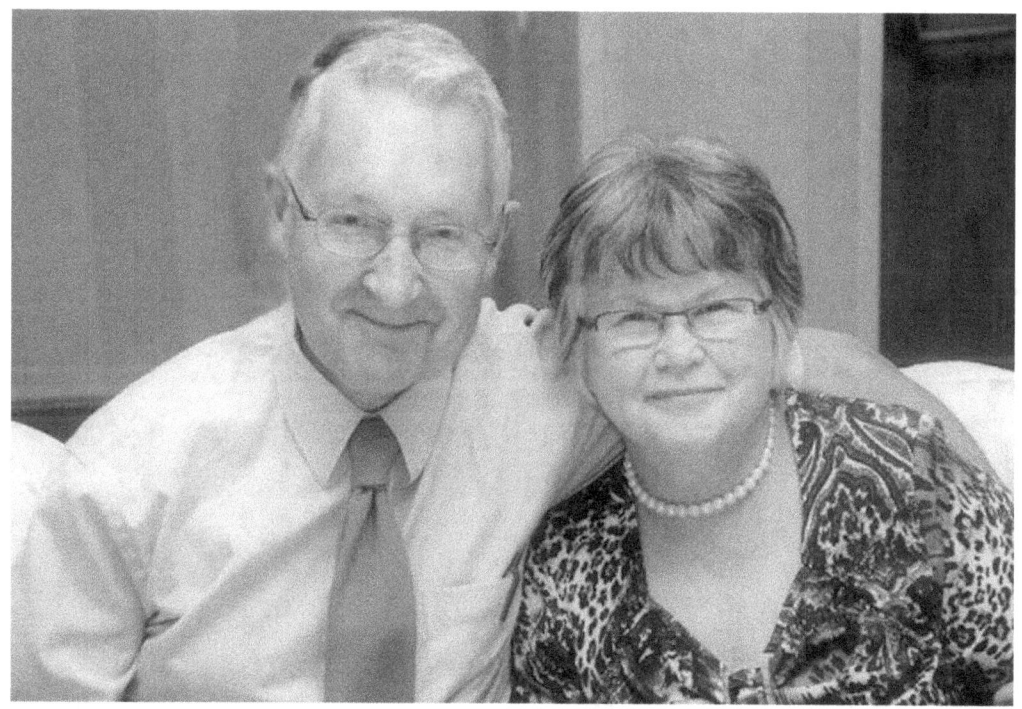

My Dad and Mom

## Parents

*"The parents exist to teach the child, but also they must learn what the child has to teach them; and the child has a very great deal to teach them"  Arnold Bennett*

Many people forget that their parents are people too with their own stories and a life full of memories. Do you know anything about your parents and who they were before they became Mom and Dad?

Questions:

When and where were your parents born?

Did they go to college?

Where did they work?

Where did your parents meet?

Tip: Ask your parents if they have any favorite photos or memories of their growing up years. You may have to ask grandparents for a copy of photos.

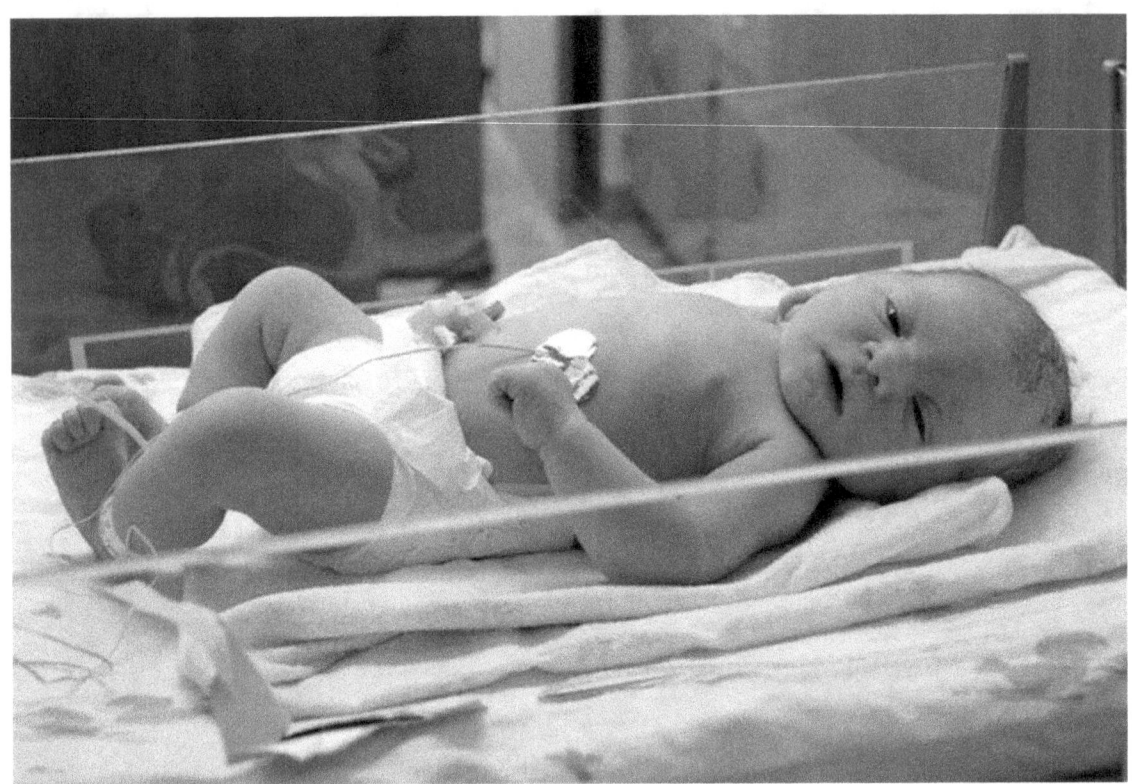

## And Then There was You

*"A new baby is like the beginning of all things, wonder, hope, a dream of possibilities."*
*Eda J LeShan*

Every new baby is the start of a new life and of course the story of you will start with when and where you were born.

Tip: If you don't have any photos of yourself as a newborn, find a photo online of the hospital you were born at to include in your story.

Questions:

Were you named for someone?

Tip: If you were named after a family member or friend of the family be sure to include a pic of you and your namesake if possible.

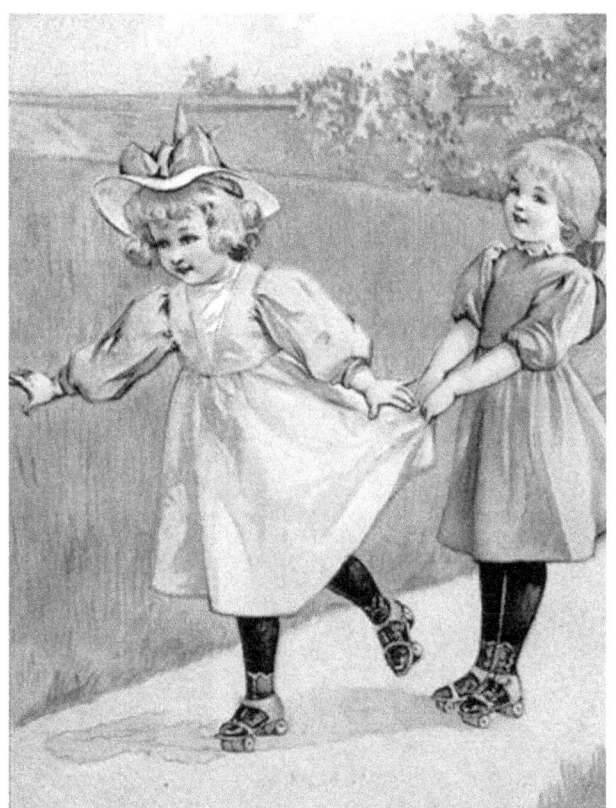

## Early Childhood

*"Play is the highest form of research."* Albert Einstein

A Child between the ages of birth and 5 years old learns so much, this is one of my favorite stages of children, I love watching them explore the world around them, they are so curious and are starting to develop their own likes and dislikes.

How much information you include in your story from this age will probably depend on how many photos you have or how good your memory is.

I don't have a lot of childhood photos so this part of my story is a little smaller than I would have liked.

## Questions:

Were you in daycare, or did your mother or other family member care for you?

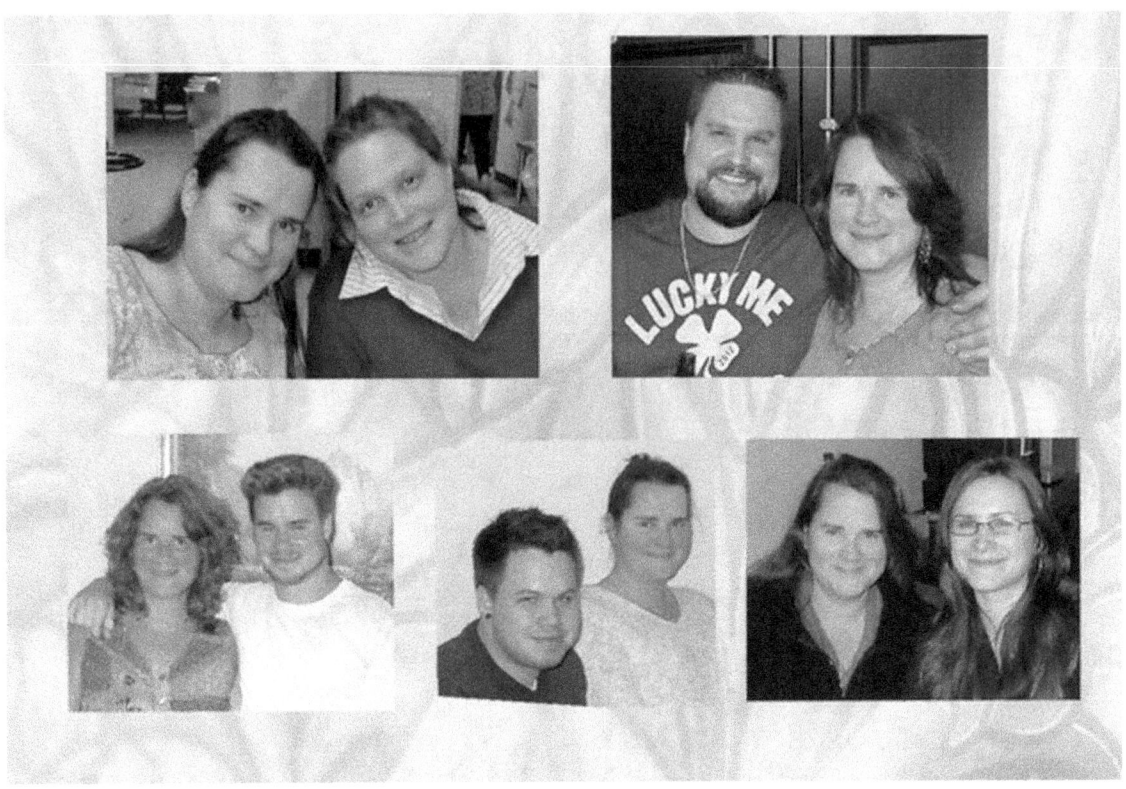

## Siblings

*"Your siblings are the only people in the world who know what it's like to have been brought up the way you were"  Betsy Cohen*

When I was growing up I sometimes wished I was an only child because our house was loud and I didn't have my own space, but I wouldn't trade any of my siblings for the world.

## Questions:

Are you an only child?(I am the oldest of 6)

If you have siblings, how many and where are you in the mix?

Tip: In my book I had a page with a photo of me and each sibling, this can be a childhood photo or older. I also added their birth date.

On another page I had photos of the siblings alone and photos of them with their family (save space if they don't have a family of their own yet).

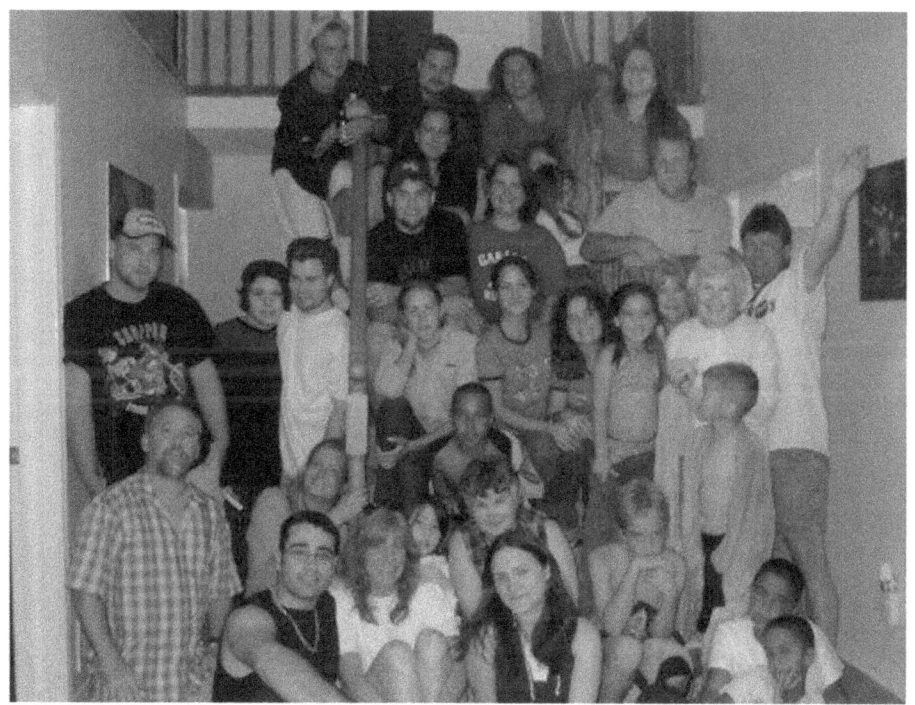

## Extended Family

*"Other things change us, but we start and end with the family. " Anthony Brandt*

Some people have a very large extended family that they only see at family reunions and there are others who have never even met their extended family.

I have a really big, fairly close family, but I live in the Southern USA and they all live in Canada so as an adult I don't see them as much as I did when I was young.

Questions:

Do you have a lot of aunts and uncles, cousins?

Did you play with your cousins, were they close friends?

Did your family have yearly reunions?

Tip: When putting together my book I found it helpful to create a page for each side of the family and write the names of my aunts and uncles on each side and how many kids they had (names included), but I didn't get into 2nd cousins etc.

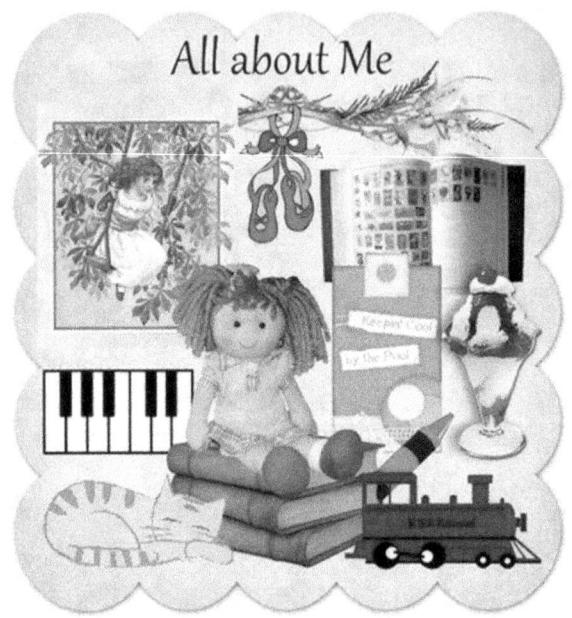

## All About Me

*"Be who you are and say what you feel, because those who mind don't matter and those who matter don't mind."  Dr. Seuss*

Your growing up years help shape the adult that you become, you develop skills, habits and tastes that often stay with you for life.

Questions:

Did you have a favorite food?

Did you have a favorite toy, blanket, teddy bear?

Did you have a favorite color that you loved to wear?

How did you spend your free time?

What were your favorite books, movies, music?

Did you do chores?

Did you go on special outings for good behavior?

Were you a healthy child or did you get sick a lot?

Were you ever in the hospital?

Were you a collector? What did you collect and do you still have your collection?

Did you have any hobbies, do you still?

Did you play an instrument?

Were you in Scouts or any other groups?

Did you take dance, karate or any other lessons?

What did you want to be when you grew up?

Did you change your mind a lot?

Tip: if you want to have the memory but don't have any photos you can use clipart or other graphics to dress up your page

## Home Sweet Home

*"Home is Where Your Story Begins"*

It was once quite common for families to live in the same home for their entire life.

The family home was often in a house passed down from generations. This is not the case for most people now.

When I was young we moved a lot and we never really had a house that would be called my childhood home.

Questions:

Did you move a lot?

What kind of home did you live in?

Did your parents own or rent?

Did you have your own room?

Tip: If you lived in lots of different houses growing up but you have no photos, you can go to google maps and capture a screenshot of the areas you lived in. You may even be able to get a photo of the exact house if it is still there.

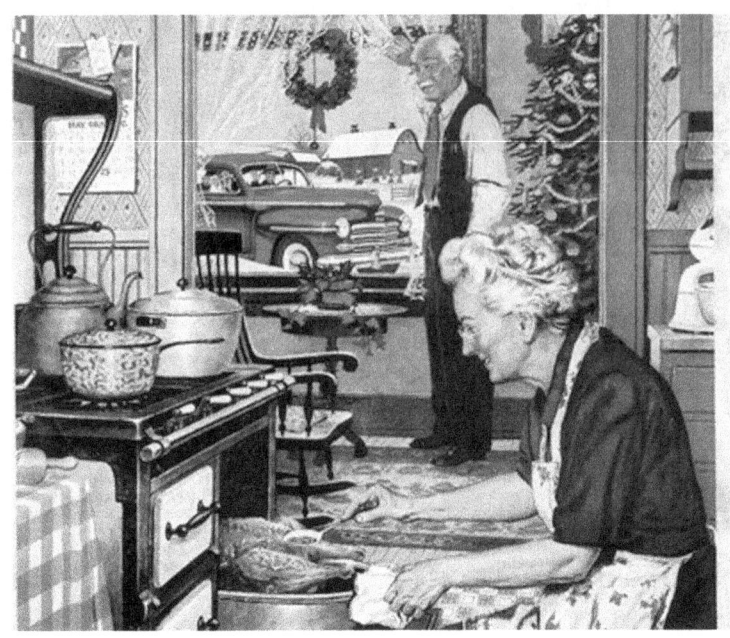

## Family Celebrations

*"What greater blessing to give thanks for at a family gathering than the family and the gathering"  Robert Brault*

Celebrations like birthdays, Christmas, Thanksgiving and other holidays are usually a time for families to get together and spend time together enjoying (or not)
each other's company and good food. Some people celebrate with sharing passed down family traditions.

<u>Questions</u>

For holidays like Christmas and Thanksgiving, did you travel?

Who was the host, who cooked?

Did you have family traditions or try something new every year?

Did your family have any special birthday traditions?

Was your birthday a bigger celebration than any other holiday?

Did you celebrate with family or just friends?

Tip: You may want to create a page for each celebration or have just one that includes them all together.

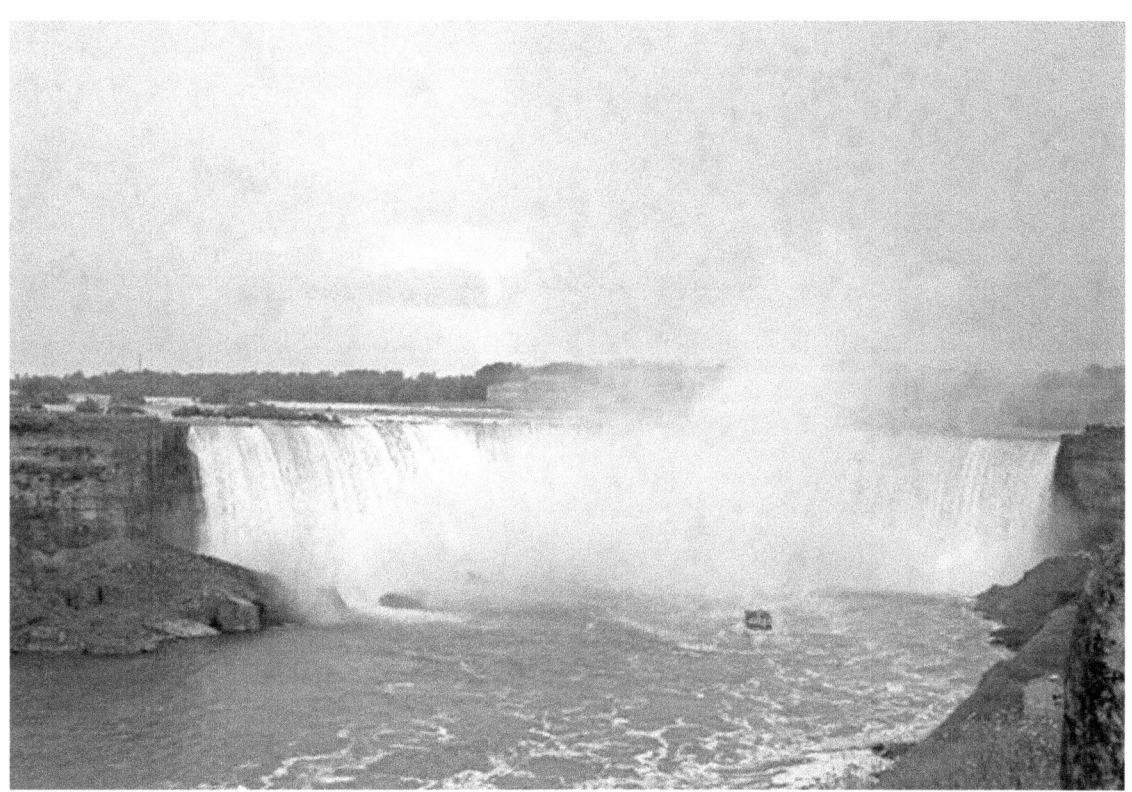

## Favorite Family Vacations
*"Are we there Yet?"*

For some people family vacation is the same time, same place every year, while for others it is lots of different places or no vacation at all. Trips to visit Grandma is a family vacation for some families (like us).

Questions:

Did your family take regular vacations?

Did you take the same trips as your parents did when they were kids?

Did you go camping?

Did you go to the lake or the beach?

How did you travel, by car, by train, by plane?

Tip: don't forget to add a great scenery shot of your favorite vacation spot. Even if you don't have any from childhood, you can always go back and get a photo. Things may have changed but then you can just add to the memory, what was different between then and now?

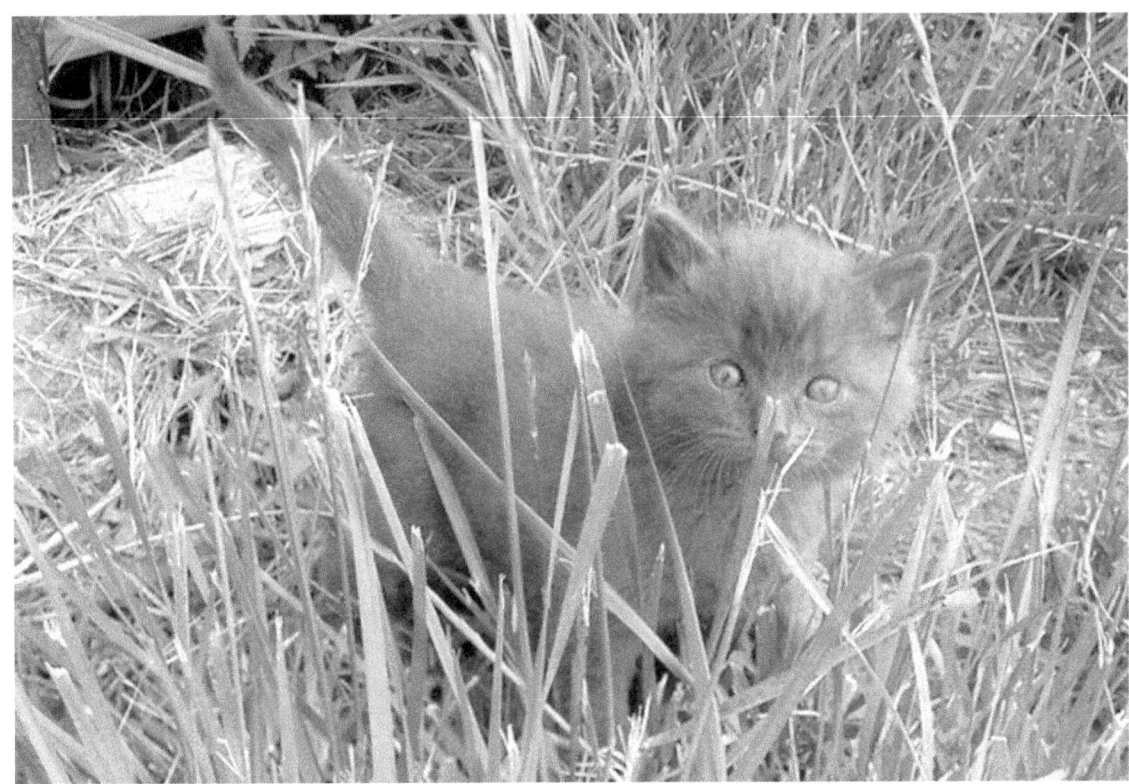

## Pets

*"Animals are such agreeable friends, they ask no questions, they pass no criticisms"* George Eliot

Pets are often more than just an animal you have, they are a member of the family, and are included in everything.

Questions:

Were you a pet family?

Did you have dogs, cats or lots of animals?

Was it your job to take care of them?

Did you have any unusual pets? (we had a pet squirrel)

Did you go to zoo's often?

Did you ever ride a horse?

Tips: You may want to create a page for childhood pets and then another page for pets you had as an adult or combine them. Don't forget to write down your pet's names.

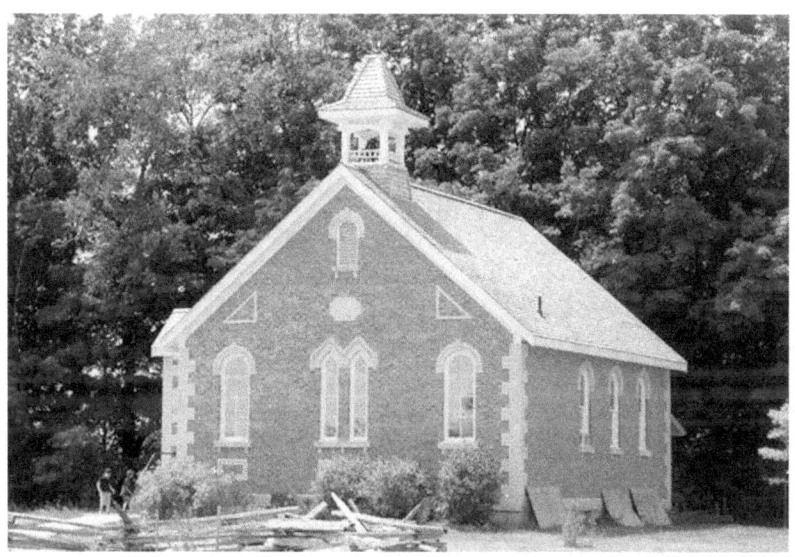

## School Years

*"Study without desire spoils the memory, and it retains nothing that it takes in."*<small>*Leonardo da Vinci*</small>

School is a huge part of childhood and your years in school can be very important to you or years you would rather forget about. Your story may include a huge section on your school years or just a short section with a few school mug shots.

Questions:

Did you like school?

Were you a good student?

Did you stay in the same school area?

Did you have a favorite subject, a worst?

Did you walk, ride the bus or did your parents drive you to school?

Did you make a lot of friends or just have a few close friends?

Were you in the School Band or Choir?

Did you play any sports?

Tips: You can get photos of the outside of your school from the school's website. Add notes of interest from saved report cards, for ex. in Kindergarten my teacher said I showed good organization skills.

# Teens

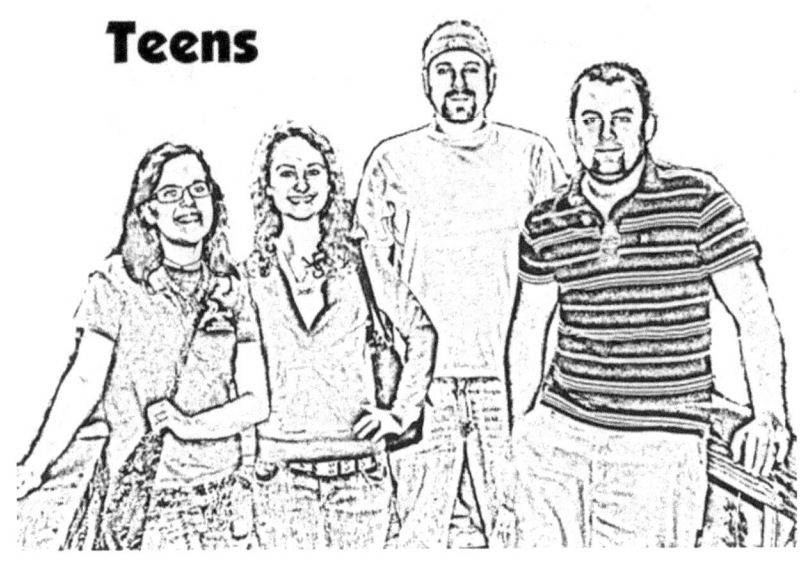

## Teen Years

*"It takes courage to grow up and become who you really are." E. E. Cummings*

It is not easy being a teen, you are dealing with so many changes. Sometimes the transition from childhood to teen is not very noticeable and other times the person becomes so different it is hard to tell that they are the same person.

Questions:

Did you have a job when you were a teen, did you get paid or was it volunteer work?

When did you learn to drive?

When did you get your 1st car and what was it?

Did you have a serious teen crush?

Did you have any wild clothing or hair styles?

Did you have a singer or movie star crush?

How did you spend your free time?

What did you dream of doing after graduation?

Tip: include some images of icons of your generation.

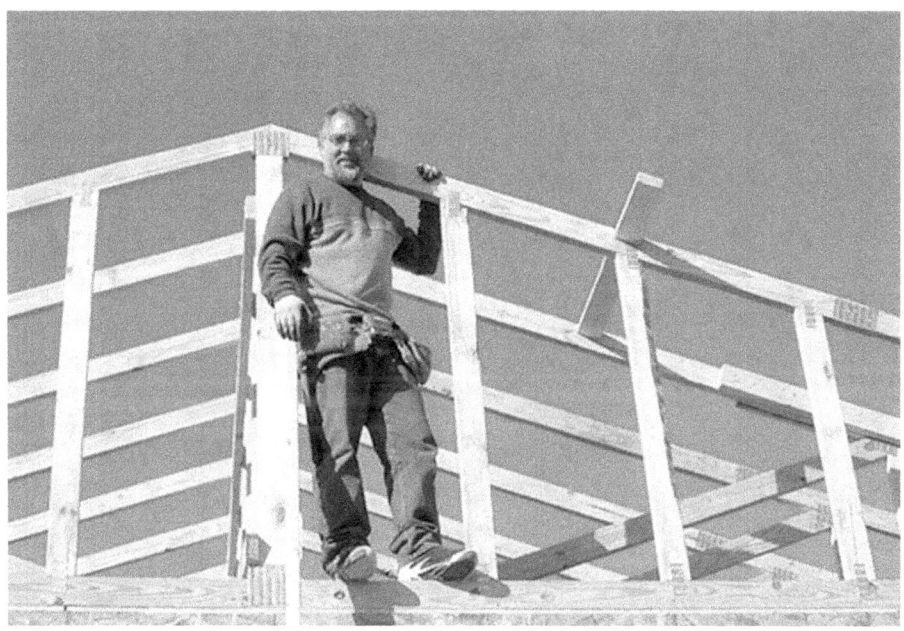

## Adult Life

*"Adults are obsolete children"  Dr. Seuss*

Adulthood brings with it a lot more freedom but also more responsibility. It is a time of new jobs, homes, friends and hobbies.

Questions:

Did you go to college, trade school, or go straight to the work force?

Or did you get married and stay home with babies?

Did you receive any awards?

Did you have one career that you loved or hated?

Were you in the military?

Did you have lots of different jobs?

Do you have any hobbies?

Have you lived thru any major world events?

Tip: most people don't have work photos, you can add a pay stub, scan an award, add a work id badge, add the logo of a company you worked for. For world events, add news photos and articles.

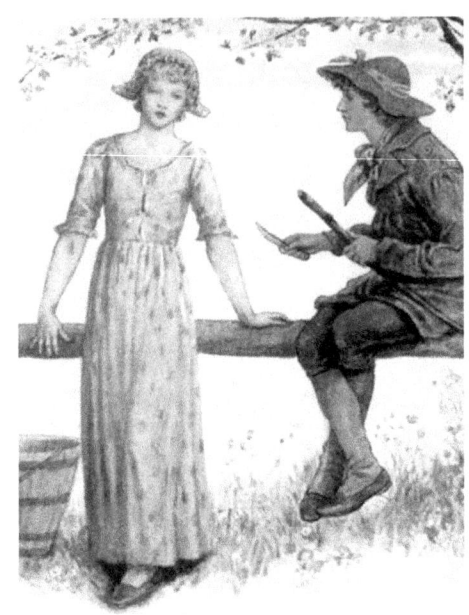

## Love and marriage

*"Where does a family start? It starts with a young man falling in love with a girl."*
*Sir Winston Churchill*

You don't have to have a spouse and family to lead a full life but for most of us that is the biggest part of our life.

Tip: don't forget to add some information and photos about your new extended family, your spouse's parent's names, their siblings and their children

Questions:

Do you believe in love at first sight?

Did you find love early in life or later?

Did you marry your childhood sweetheart or someone else years later?

Did you marry young or older?

Did you have a fancy wedding or something simple, or did you elope?

Do you enjoy homemaking, or do you and your spouse take care of the house together?

Do you enjoy cooking or does your spouse cook?

Do you and your spouse do any hobbies or sports together?

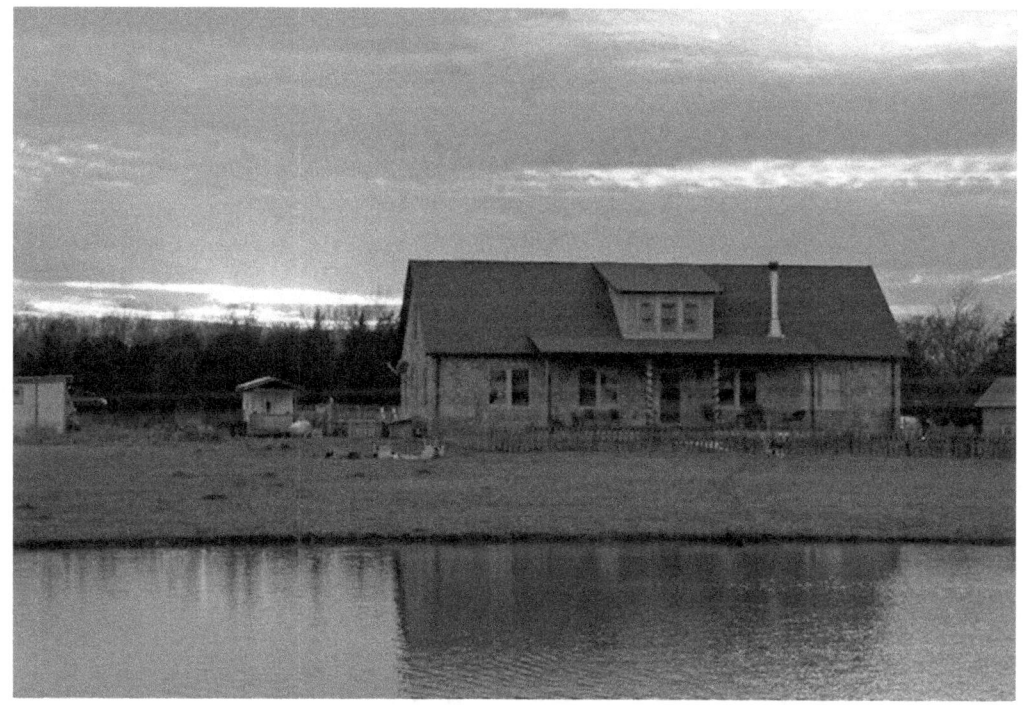

## Homes
*"Where thou art, that is Home." Emily Dickinson*

A home is not just four walls and a roof, it can be a tent, a trailer, an apartment, or a large or small house. It is important to make any space you are living in your home. Your home doesn't have to look like a showhouse, make it yours, filled with things you use and love.

Tip: if you don't have a photo of a home you lived in, google search the address and you may find a photo of the home on a Real Estate listing or on Google Maps. You can also add a satellite overview of the property.

Questions:

Are you a renter or do you own a home?

Do you move a lot?

Have you lived in other states?

Have you lived in another country?

Do you like to decorate?

Do you have flower or food gardens?

Have you ever built a home?
Are you a do it yourself home improvement person?

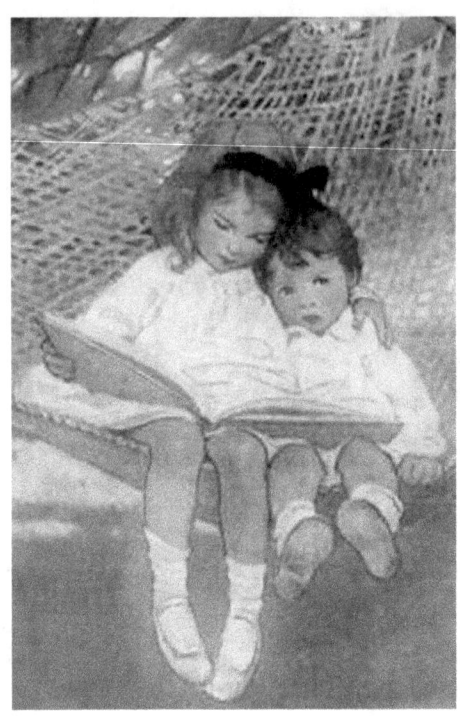

## Children

*"While we try to teach our children all about life, Our children teach us what life is all about."*
*Angela Schwindt*

In this section you may want to just add a little bit about your children. Even though your children are a big part of who you are, this is not a book about them. They probably fill all the other photo albums in the house.

Tip: have a page for each child with their name and birthday and some of your favorite photos of them and have a page with some favorite family photos. Don't forget to caption the photos with the year.

Questions:

When you were growing up did you want children?

How many children do you have?

Did you spend a lot of time doing extra activities like dance, sports and music lessons?

Did you homeschool your children?

Were you involved in school activities?

Tip: have a page with each child and their new spouse (use their wedding photo and don't forget to write their spouses full name).

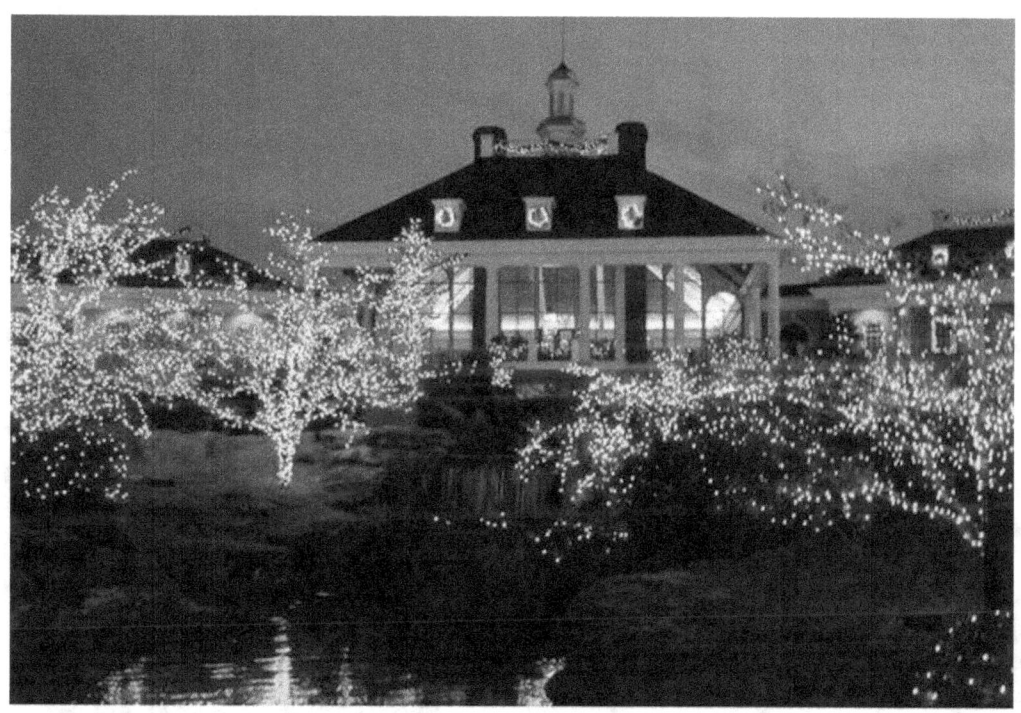

## New Family Celebrations

*"Blessed is the season which engages the whole world in a conspiracy of love"*
*Hamilton Wright Mabie*

After marriage, many people have trouble figuring out how to celebrate the holidays. They are now torn between 2 different families and family traditions and
wanting to spend time together and start their own family traditions.

Question:

How do you celebrate a holiday, is it a big deal with family and friends or just a quiet time at home?

Do you like to cook and decorate?

Do you continue any family traditions?

Have you made any new traditions?

Do you travel and spend the holidays with different sides of the family?

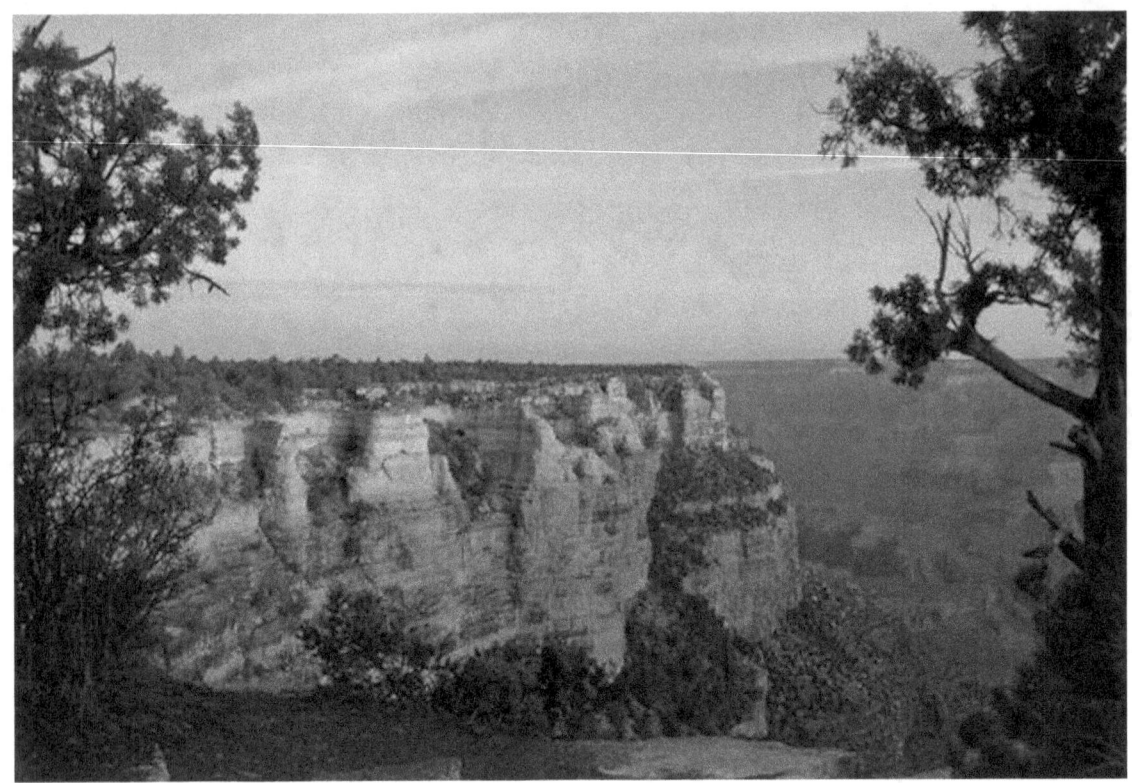

## Vacations

*"Be an explorer. The universe is filled with wonder and magical things" Flavia*

Family vacations are a time to be together without the distractions of everyday life.

Your family may go to the same place at the same time every year or explore different places every time. For our family most of our vacations were going to Canada to visit extended family.

Questions:

Do you like to travel?

What is the best vacation you've ever had?

What was the longest road trip?

What was the worst trip?

Did you ever travel out of the country?

Tip: create a page of different vacation spots.

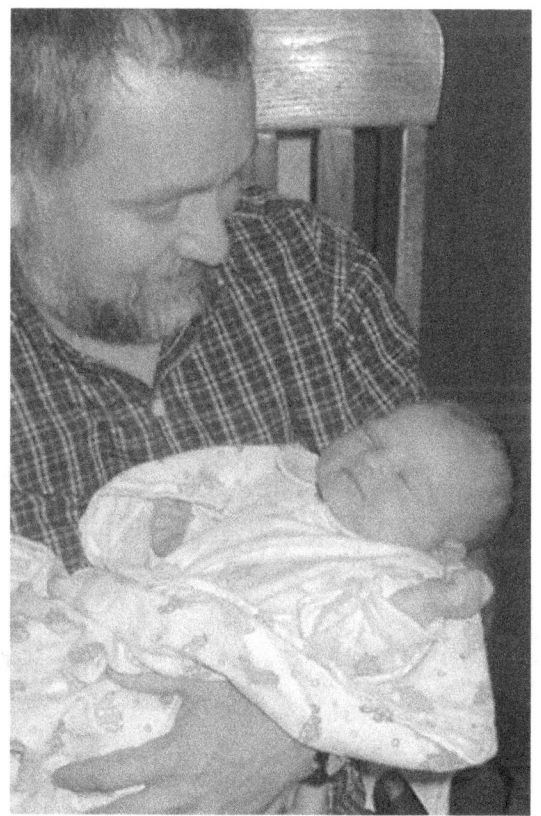

## Grandchildren

*"Perfect love sometimes does not come until the first grandchild."* *Welsh Proverb*

There is nothing that can prepare you for the feelings you have when you become a grandparent. It is different from being a parent, there is not the responsibility and more time to love and enjoy them.

Tip: when doing my book I created a collage style page and showed all the grandchildren with their names and birthdays and left space for more children.
Add a generational photo if possible or create a page with a photo of each generation.

Questions:

How many grandchildren do you have?

Do your grandchildren live close by?

Do you babysit your grandchildren or just visit with them?

Did you take your grandchildren to places you took your own children?

How many generations of your family are still alive?

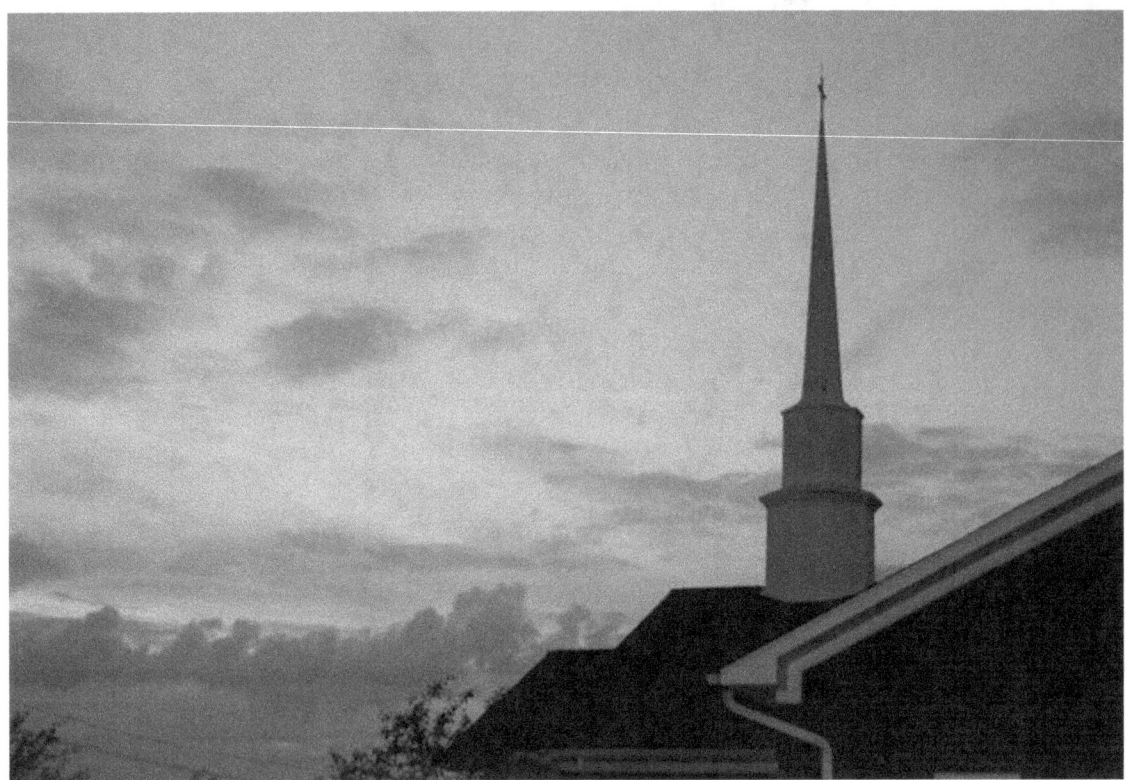

## Religion and beliefs

*"Life without faith in something is too narrow a space to live"* George Spalding

Being a part of a church is an important part of life to many people and there are lots of different church functions that you may have photos of.

Questions:

Did you go to the same church as your parents?

Are you a member of a church or do you go visit different churches?

Does your church family have picnics or other get togethers?

Were you baptized or dedicated?

Tips: add a photo of your church from their website and include their statement of faith.

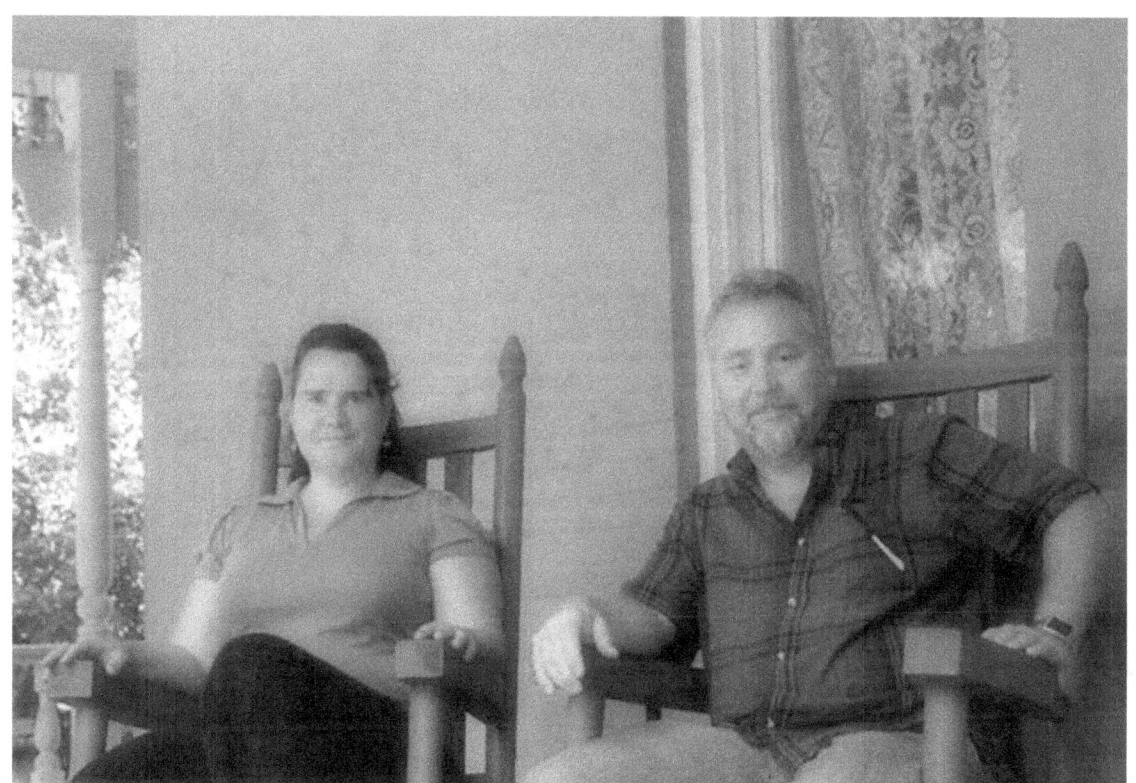

# Retirement

*"Don't simply retire from something; have something to retire to"*  *Harry Emerson Fosdick*

Retirement for most people is more than just quitting work and sitting in a rocking chair on the front porch. It can be a time to start a 2nd career, finish projects, go back to school, travel and spend more time with loved ones.

Of course your retirement may involve sitting on the porch in a rocking chair (it is such a great place to read a book).

No matter what your retirement looks like to you, having a reduced stress level and a more relaxed schedule is usually what people are looking forward to.

Tip: you may not be at this stage of life yet (I'm not) but you can create a page with images of things you would like to do when you retire. Show your bucket list.
(things you would like to see and do).

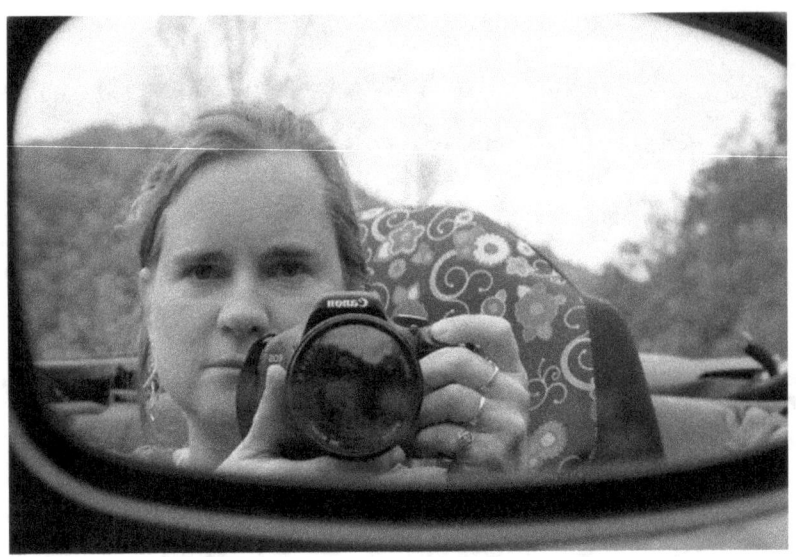

## Your life Now

*"Yesterday is history. Tomorrow is a mystery. Today is a gift. That's why we call it the present".*
*Babatunde Olatunji*

Some of Us (like me) spend most of our lives taking care of other people. Our photo albums are full of friends and family and their accomplishments. It is important to celebrate you and the things you Love and Do that make you unique.

Tip: Include current photos of yourself and don't forget to date them. Create a page of your current home town.

Questions:

Do you have a unique sense of style or hairstyle?

Do you have a favorite hobby?

Are you a big reader?

Do you like computers and other electronics?

Are you a flower or nature lover?

Have you had any kind of life changing illness or injury?

Are you dealing with life changes like empty nest or parents living with you?

Do you enjoy traveling?

Have you started a new business?

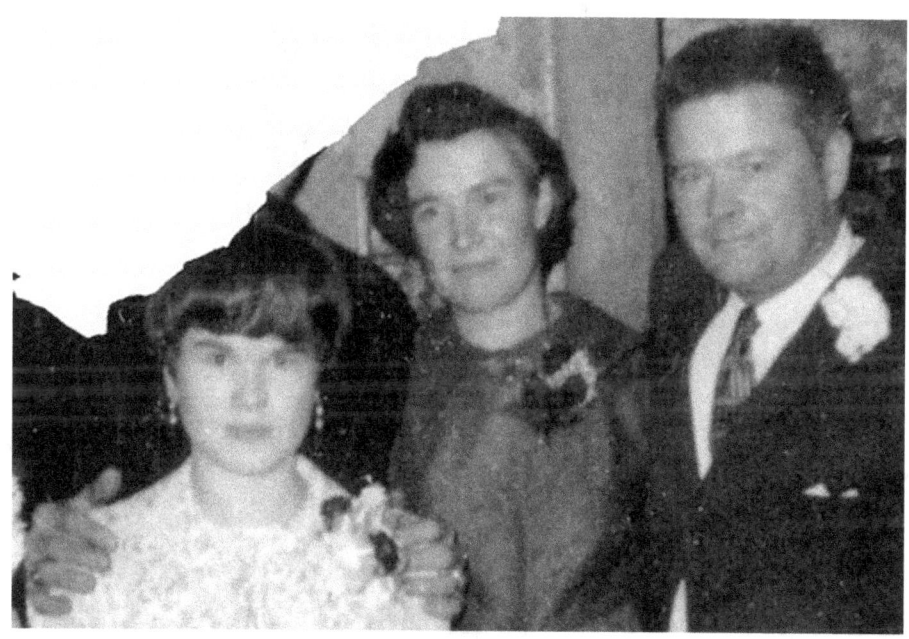

# Dealing with uncomfortable parts of your story

*"If you cannot get rid of the family skeleton, you may as well make it dance."*
*George Bernard Shaw*

Life is not always perfect and sometimes you have parts of your story that are just icky. I'm not talking about small stuff, like you stepped in dog yuck with your new
shoes on, but real life changing things, like an unexpected family death or a messy divorce.

If you want to go into detail about these things in your story then do so, but remember you are probably sharing your story with other people and you don't want to make them uncomfortable by turning your story into a private diary.

You can just lightly touch on facts without getting into all the details or feelings and move on.

It is important to make a note of these parts of your story because people will notice things, such as having a different dad in photos.

Documenting does not mean you need to give importance to negative stuff. For example, my father left when I was little. I could make a big negative story about it
or just choose to focus on the positive and say my mother remarried and I had a new Dad and soon after lots of new siblings.

You don't have to make your story look like it is perfect and nothing bad every happens. Be genuine, but focus on the good in life. Even if you feel like there are more uncomfortable stories than happy ones, usually it is because the yucky stuff is more dramatic and consuming than the every day little things that are easy to overlook.

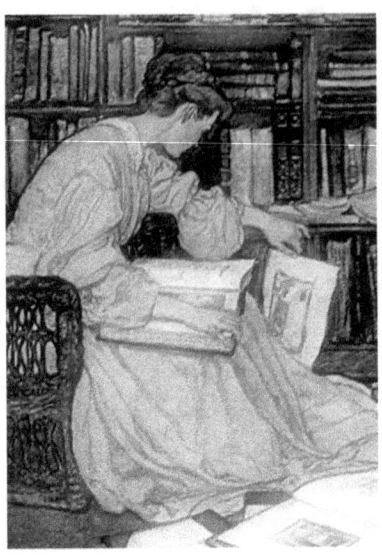

## Planning and Creating your Book

*"The best time for planning a book is while you're doing the dishes."*  *Agatha Christie*

When putting together your book you will want to do a little bit of planning and organizing before you get started. Treat it like a real book, have a nice introduction, dedication page, and you can even create an artistic title page for each chapter.

Your story will be more interesting if you can create it with a mix of photos, stories and documents. Your photos tell a story but they can't tell the whole story so you do need to write a little.

Tip: create a cover page using your favorite image (don't forget to name and date the photo).

Questions:

Will you be doing a scrapbook style album, a regular photo album, or an online book that you can create and print?

Do you like ornate paper scrapbook pages or digital scrapbooks or do you want to mix them up?

What size book are you going to use?

Do you know the names and all the information for other family members that you want to add?

Do you have the names of the schools you attended, places you worked etc?

Tip: I like to use a standard 8.5 x11 binder style album with white cardstock and clear plastic page protectors. This allows me to easily add pages anywhere.

That brings me to the photos. Do you know what photos you want to use (if you take as many photos as I do there is no way you could use even half of them in your story).
Will you pick your photos 1st and then create your pages or would you find it easier to create an outline and know what pages you want and choose your photos that way?

Organize your photos. Choose the best but try to choose ones that show character and emotion and that help tell the story you are trying to get across. Get rid of bad ones and duplicates, but remember a blurry memory is better than none. If the only photo you have of a story you want to tell is awful, use it anyway.

Tip: record yourself showing your photos to someone. Write down what you said about the photo that needed more explanation. Knowing what you want to include in your book will make it much easier for you to start and finish your story.

## Personalizing and Adding Other Elements

*"Creativity is inventing,experimenting, growing, taking risks, breaking rules, making mistakes, and having fun."* Mary Lou Cook

For some people personalizing their pages is a fun part and you may want to create scrapbook style pages using paper, lace, stickers and other embellishments. For others it may be something you completely skip and just have simple pages with photos and your writing. There is no right or wrong way, you can be as creative as you want when putting together your story. You can also add your photos and writing and go back later and add embellishments.

Tip: You can decorate your page with old postcards, movie tickets or other memorabilia.

## Photo Tips

The more you know about photography the better your photos and your books will look. You can improve the look of old photos with simple adjustments in a photo editing program.

Just cropping some of the extra space and brightening an image will improve it. Learning just a few simple tips can help your photos look better.

<u>Tips:</u>

You don't need a new camera, learn how to use the one you have, read your manual

Zoom in and get closer to the subject

Avoid trash cans etc. in your background

Try to take your photos in natural light instead of using a flash

Take lots of photos, with digital there is no reason to take just one photo, practice will help you improve

Relax and take your time

Try different angles

Think about what story you are trying to tell with the photo

Focus on eyes

Don't compare your photos to others, compare your photos to your own, you will see improvements

If you love photography, be sure to join me on my blog www.photosbybridget.net
I talk about capturing life and share simple photo and scrapbooking tips and my own experiences improving my photography skills.

# My Page Examples

I created very simple pages (8.5 x 11) I do some with paper but I create most of them in digital (created in Photoshop elements and then had them printed)

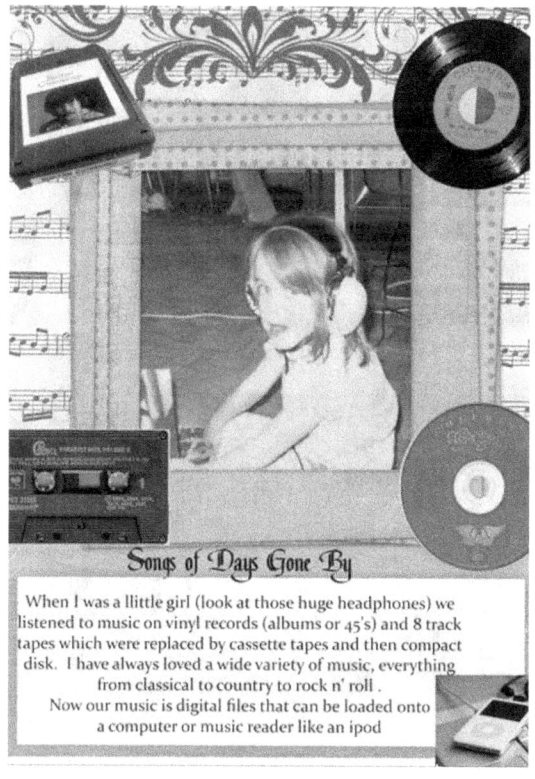

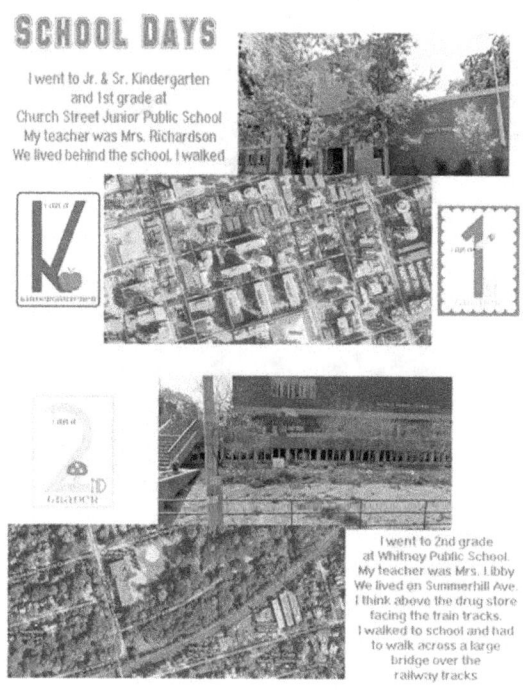

# ANCESTORS

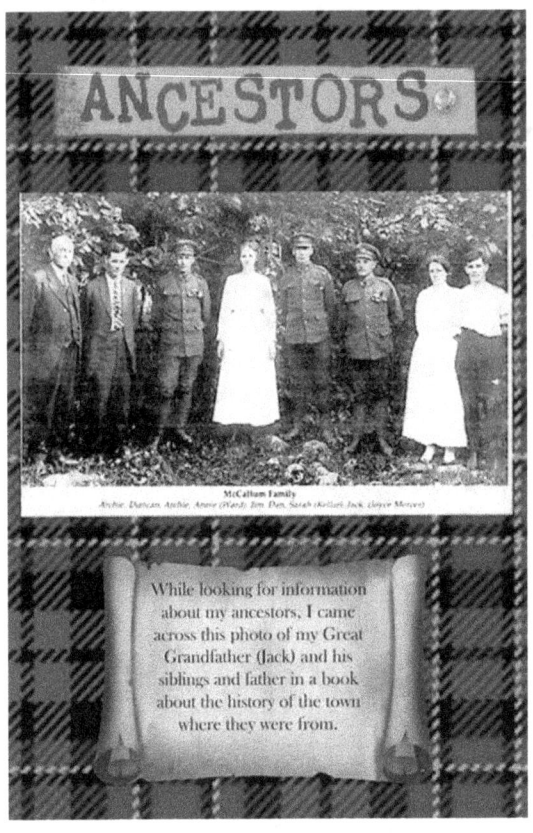

**McCallum Family**
*Archie, Duncan, Archie, Annie (Hand) Jim, Dan, Sarah (Keller) Jack, (Joyce Meyer)*

While looking for information about my ancestors, I came across this photo of my Great Grandfather (Jack) and his siblings and father in a book about the history of the town where they were from.

## Great Grandparents

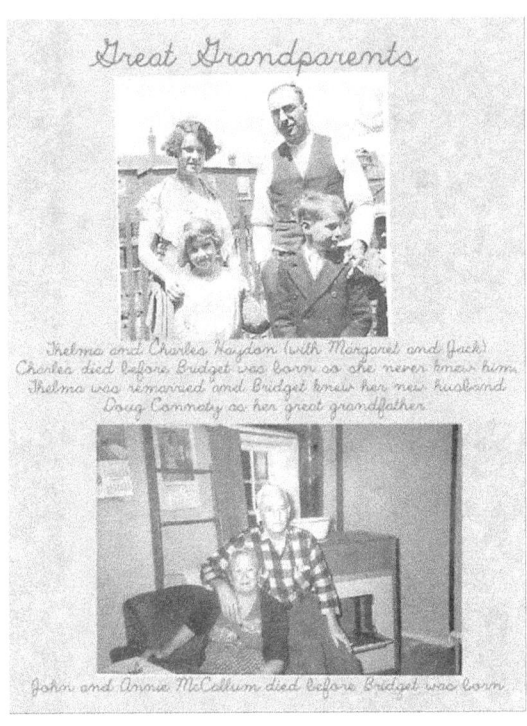

Thelma and Charles Haydon (with Margaret and Jack)
Charles died before Bridget was born so she never knew him.
Thelma was remarried and Bridget knew her new husband
Doug Connoly as her great grandfather

John and Annie McCallum died before Bridget was born

## Conclusion

You can start telling your story at any stage of life and just add to it, you don't have to wait until you are old to start. Whenever I am feeling nostalgic there is nothing I like better than pulling out a photo album and seeing my memories displayed, plus my children have enjoyed sharing photos of their childhood with their spouses and children.

Having a book of your life in photos is much easier to share with people than overwhelming them with a huge stack of family photo albums.

"Amazing things happen to people. Then they die. If no one remembers their stories, the memory of who they were and what they did blurs, like watercolor paintings left in the rain. Until, finally, nothing is left on the canvas."  Cherie Bennett

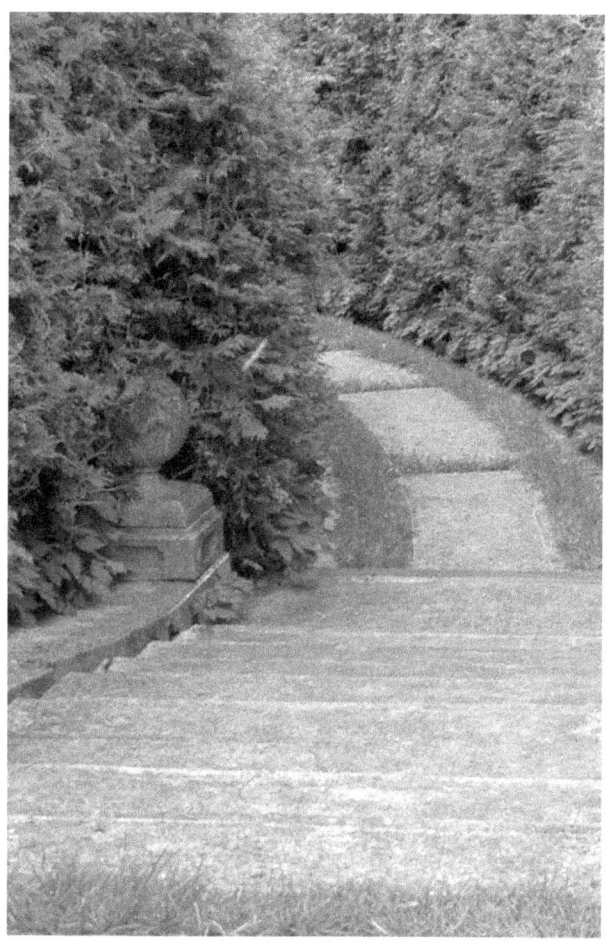

Enjoy your trip down memory lane, and don't forget to stop by my blog at
http://photosbybridget.net

I would love to hear from you and let me know if you have any questions or comments.

Bridget

www.ingramcontent.com/pod-product-compliance
Lightning Source LLC
Chambersburg PA
CBHW081408170526
45166CB00010B/3252